MAY   2014

CR

Cool Western Cooking

Easy and Fun Regional Recipes

Alex Kuskowski

visit us at www.abdopublishing.com

Published by ABDO Publishing Company, a division of ABDO, P.O. Box 398166, Minneapolis, Minnesota 55439. Copyright © 2014 by Abdo Consulting Group, Inc. International copyrights reserved in all countries. No part of this book may be reproduced in any form without written permission from the publisher. Super SandCastle™ is a trademark and logo of ABDO Publishing Company.

Printed in the United States of America, North Mankato, Minnesota
062013
092013

Editor: Liz Salzmann
Content Developer: Nancy Tuminelly
Cover and Interior Design and Production:
Colleen Dolphin, Mighty Media, Inc.
Food Production: Desirée Bussiere
Photo Credits: Colleen Dolphin, Shutterstock

The following manufacturers/names appearing in this book are trademarks: Allens®, Carnation®, Gold Medal®, Heinz®, La Preferida®, Nestle®, Old El Paso®, Swanson®

Library of Congress Cataloging-in-Publication Data

Kuskowski, Alex.
  Cool Western cooking : easy and fun regional recipes / Alex Kuskowski.
      p. cm. -- (Cool USA cooking)
  Audience: 008-012.
  Includes bibliographical references and index.
  ISBN 978-1-61783-833-0 (alk. paper)
  1. Cooking, American--Western style--Juvenile literature.
  I. Title.
  TX715.2.W47K875 2014
  641.5978--dc23
                                        2013001905

Safety First!

Some recipes call for activities or ingredients that require caution. If you see these symbols ask an adult for help!

HOT STUFF!
This recipe requires the use of a stove or oven. Always use pot holders when handling hot objects.

SUPER SHARP!
This recipe includes the use of a sharp **utensil** such as a knife or grater.

NUT ALERT!
Some people can get very sick if they eat nuts. If you are cooking with nuts, let people know!

Cuisine Cooking

Each regional recipe can have a lot of **versions**. Many are **unique** to the cook. The recipes in this book are meant to give you just a taste of regional cooking. If you want to learn more about one kind of cooking, go to your local library or search online. There are many great recipes to try!

Contents

Discover Western Eats!

"Yee-Haw!" Grab your boots and your cowboy hat. It's time to explore the hearty foods of the American West. It's rough, **outdoorsy**, and always too good to pass up!

Western cooking is a tasty mix of Native American farming, Mexican recipes, and American cowboy know-how. Many Western dishes are full of vegetables that have been grown by native tribes for hundreds of years. Mexican foods such as tortillas, **burritos**, and chilies are a part of many meals.

There is a lot to learn about foods from the American West. Use the recipes in this book to have your own feast. Try them all, or make up your own. Grab a chef's hat, it's time for a cooking adventure!

Learn About the Wild West

Regional cooking has a lot to do with where the ingredients and recipes are from. Every region has its own **culture**. What do you know about Western culture and food?

New Mexico

New Mexico has a state cookie that reflects its strong Native American and Mexican **heritage**. It's the biscochito.

Arizona

The chimichanga is a **versatile**, popular dish from Arizona. It can be served for dinner or **dessert**.

Colorado

Many Native Americans live in this area of the West. One of their most popular traditional foods is tasty fry bread.

Nevada

Nevada has been an important state for ranchers and cattle. A meal they eat a lot is huevos rancheros. That's Spanish for "rancher's eggs."

Montana

When people began moving West to states such as Montana, beef **jerky** was a popular food. It lasted a long time and tasted **delicious**.

Utah

Scones in Utah are fried rather than baked. It's a tasty local specialty.

Idaho

Idaho has a lot of potatoes. Almost every **grocery store** in the country has potatoes from an Idaho farm. Potatoes are used in all sorts of regional dishes.

Wyoming

Wyoming is also known as "the Cowboy State." It's well known for cowboys, including Butch Cassidy and Buffalo Bill. Cowboys often ate potatoes, beans, dried meat, fruit, and tea.

The Basics

Ask Permission

Before you cook, ask **permission** to use the kitchen, cooking tools, and ingredients. If you'd like to do something yourself, say so. Just remember to be safe. If you would like help, ask for it. Always ask for help using a stove or oven.

Be Prepared

- Be organized. Knowing where everything is makes cooking easier and safer.

- Read the directions all the way through before you start. Remember to follow the directions in order.

- The most important ingredient in great cooking is preparation! Set out all your ingredients before starting.

Be Neat and Clean

- Start with clean hands, clean tools, and a clean work surface.

- Tie back long hair so it stays out of the food.

- Wear comfortable clothing. Roll up long sleeves.

Be Smart, Be Safe

- Never work in the kitchen if you are home alone.

- Always have an adult close by for hot jobs, such as using the oven or the stove.

- Have an adult around when using a sharp tool, such as a knife or grater. Always be careful when using them!

- Remember to turn pot handles toward the back of the stove. That way you won't accidentally knock them over.

Cool Cooking Terms

Peel
Peel means to remove the skin, often with a peeler.

Chop
Chop means to cut into small pieces.

Boil
Boil means to heat liquid until it begins to bubble.

Dice / Cube
Dice and *cube* mean to cut something into small squares.

Slice
Slice means to cut food into pieces of the same thickness.

Shred
Shred means to tear or cut into small pieces.

Drain
Drain means to pour out all the excess liquid.

Mince
Mince means to cut or chop into very small pieces.

The Tool Box

Here are some of the tools that you'll need for the recipes in this book.

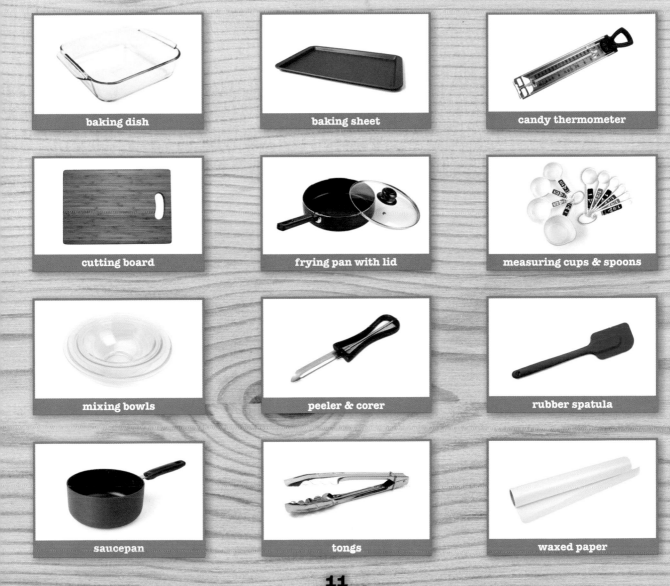

baking dish

baking sheet

candy thermometer

cutting board

frying pan with lid

measuring cups & spoons

mixing bowls

peeler & corer

rubber spatula

saucepan

tongs

waxed paper

The Ingredients

Here are some of the ingredients that you'll need for the recipes in this book.

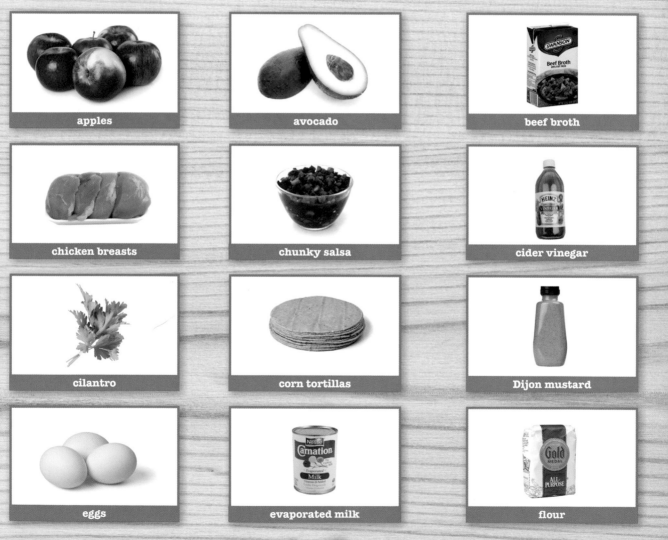

apples	avocado	beef broth
chicken breasts	chunky salsa	cider vinegar
cilantro	corn tortillas	Dijon mustard
eggs	evaporated milk	flour

flour tortillas

green chilies

ground beef

honey

lettuce

onion

pecans

pinto beans

pita bread

potatoes

red beans

red cabbage

refried beans

tomatoes

white hominy

13

Huevos Rancheros

A Mexican classic with a Western kick!

Makes 4 servings

Ingredients

2 tablespoons butter
4 eggs
4 corn tortillas
1 cup refried beans
1 cup chunky salsa
1 cup grated cheddar cheese
¼ cup chopped cilantro
2 avocados, sliced

Tools

large frying pan with lid
paper towels
measuring cups
sharp knife
cutting board
grater
spatula

*hot!
*sharp!

1. Put the butter in the frying pan. Melt it over medium heat for 30 seconds. Crack the eggs into the pan one at a time. Cook for 2 minutes. Do not stir. Cover the eggs. Cook for 1 more minute. Take the pan off the heat.

2. Place each tortilla between two paper towels. Microwave each tortilla for 10 to 15 seconds.

3. Place each tortilla on a plate. Spread ¼ cup beans and ¼ cup salsa on each one.

4. Put a fried egg on each tortilla. Sprinkle cheese and cilantro on top. Serve with avocado slices.

Arizona Beef Stew

A warm stew to brighten your day!

Makes 4 servings

Ingredients

- 1 pound ground beef
- 1 cup diced onion
- 2 teaspoons minced garlic
- 1 teaspoon chili powder
- 1 teaspoon ground cumin
- 2 cups peeled and diced potato
- 1½ cups white hominy
- 8-ounce can peeled tomatoes, chopped
- 1½ cups beef broth
- ¼ teaspoon salt
- ¼ teaspoon black pepper

Tools

- large saucepan
- mixing spoon
- sharp knife
- cutting board
- measuring cups
- measuring spoons

*hot!
*sharp!

1   Put the ground beef in the saucepan. Cook over medium heat. Stir constantly.

   2   Cook 10 minutes, or until all the pink is gone. Add the onion, garlic, and chili powder. Stir and cook for 7 more minutes.

3   Turn heat to medium-low. Add the remaining ingredients. Stir and cook 2 minutes.

4   Cover. Cook over low heat for 90 minutes.

Even Cooler!

Give this dish an extra kick like they do out West! Add chopped green chilies, jalapeno peppers, or adobo seasonings.

Red Bean Pita Salad

Zippy flavors make this a super salad!

Makes 6 servings

Ingredients

3 pieces of pita bread
2 cups sliced red cabbage
12 lettuce leaves, sliced
1 can red beans
1 cup diced tomato
¼ cup diced green chilies
1 cup frozen corn
½ cup diced zucchini
½ cup diced yellow squash
¼ cup chopped onion
1 tablespoon minced cilantro
2 tablespoons lime juice
3 tablespoons olive oil
3 tablespoons cider vinegar
3 tablespoons Dijon mustard
2 tablespoons honey
1 teaspoon minced garlic
¼ teaspoon salt
¼ teaspoon ground cumin
⅛ teaspoons cayenne pepper

Tools

baking sheet
pot holders
small bowl
sharp knife
cutting board
measuring cups & spoons
large mixing bowl & mixing spoon
large serving bowl
plastic zipper bag
serving spoon & fork

1 Preheat the oven to 375 degrees. Split all pitas in half. Place them on the baking sheet. Bake for 10 minutes. Take them out and let them cool.

2 Break the pita halves into bite-size pieces. Put them in a small bowl.

3 Put the cabbage, lettuce, red beans, tomatoes, green chilies, corn, zucchini, squash, and onion in a large mixing bowl. Mix with your hands. Sprinkle the cilantro and 1 tablespoon lime juice on top. Stir with a spoon. Put the salad in the serving bowl.

4 Put the olive oil, cider vinegar, Djion mustard, honey, garlic, salt, cumin, cayenne pepper, and 1 tablespoon lime juice in the plastic bag. Close the bag. Squeeze the bag to mix the dressing.

5 Put pita pieces on the salad. Pour dressing on top. Toss with a serving spoon and fork. Serve right away for a quick, healthy lunch!

*hot!
*sharp!

Southwestern Chicken Enchiladas

A mouthwatering specialty for all!

Makes 10 to 12 servings

Ingredients

non-stick cooking spray

2 chicken breasts

8 ounces cream cheese

2 cups salsa

15.5-ounce can pinto beans, drained

6 large corn tortillas

2 cups grated pepper-Jack cheese

¼ cup chopped cilantro

Tools

baking dish

measuring cups

grater

saucepan

fork

large mixing bowl

mixing spoon

spoon

pot holders

*hot!
*sharp!

1 Preheat the oven to 350 degrees. Coat the baking dish with cooking spray.

2 Put 4 cups water in the saucepan. Bring to a boil over high heat. Add the chicken breasts. Turn the heat to medium-low. Cook for 15 minutes. Turn off the stove. Take the chicken out of the pan. Let it cool. Shred the cooked chicken with a fork.

3 Put the cream cheese and salsa in a mixing bowl. Microwave 20 seconds. Then stir. Repeat until the cheese is melted. Add the chicken and pinto beans. Stir well.

4 Lay out the tortillas. Put some of the cream cheese mixture on each one. Roll up the tortillas. Put them in the baking dish. Sprinkle the pepper-jack cheese evenly over the top.

5 Bake for 30 minutes. Take the baking dish out of the oven. Sprinkle cilantro on the enchiladas.

Fantastic Fry Bread

Serve up this tasty snack anytime!

Makes about 10 pieces

Ingredients

3 cups flour
1 tablespoon baking powder
½ teaspoon salt
2 cups cooking oil

Tools

measuring cups
measuring spoons
large mixing bowl
mixing spoon
plastic wrap
large frying pan
tongs
paper towels

*hot!

1 Put the flour, baking powder, and salt in a large mixing bowl. Stir.

2 Slowly add ½ cup of warm water. Mix with your hands by squeezing the dough. Add ¾ cups of warm water. Mix with your hands. Squeeze and mix the dough until it is soft. Cover the bowl with plastic wrap. Let it sit for 15 minutes.

3 Roll three tablespoons of dough into a ball. Flatten the ball. Make it as flat as possible. Repeat until you've used all of the dough.

4 Put the cooking oil in the frying pan. Heat until it is bubbling. Put the dough circles in three at a time. Cook them until bubbles appear on top of the dough. Flip them over with the tongs. Cook for another 30 seconds.

5 Put the fry bread on paper towels to cool. Serve with jam or honey.

Smooth & Spicy Chili con Queso

This dip is a crowd pleaser!

Makes 8 servings

Ingredients

1 cup chopped onion

1 tablespoon minced garlic

2 tablespoons butter

½ cup milk

4-ounce can chopped green chilies, drained

1 tablespoon flour

½ cup diced tomato

¼ cup chopped cilantro

2 cups cubed cheddar cheese

2 cups cubed Monterey Jack cheese

¼ cup sour cream

1 tablespoon ground cumin

1 tablespoon cayenne pepper

Tools

sharp knife

cutting board

large saucepan

mixing spoon

*hot!
*sharp!

1. Put the onion, garlic, and butter in a saucepan. Heat over medium heat. Cook and stir for 5 minutes.

2. Add the milk, chilies, and flour. Cook and stir constantly for 5 more minutes.

3. Turn heat to low. Add tomatoes and cilantro.

4. Add the cheese ¼ cup at a time. Stir until the cheese is melted before adding more. Repeat until all the cheese is melted in.

5. Turn off heat. Stir in sour cream, cumin, and cayenne pepper. Serve right away with your favorite tortilla chips!

Cinnamon Apple Chimichangas

Try this desert treat for a dessert twist!

Makes 6 servings

Ingredients

3 apples
½ cup butter
½ cup brown sugar
1 teaspoon ground cinnamon
3 flour tortillas

Tools

peeler & corer
sharp knife
cutting board
measuring cups
measuring spoons
2 frying pans
mixing bowl
basting brush

*hot!
*sharp!

1   Core the apples. Then peel and dice them.

2   Put ¼ cup butter in a frying pan. Melt over medium-high heat. Add the brown sugar and cinnamon. Stir until sugar becomes smooth. This takes about 5 minutes.

③   Add the apples. Cook and stir 5 minutes. Remove from heat. Put the apple mixture in a bowl.

④   Melt ¼ cup of butter in the microwave. Brush both sides of each tortilla with butter.

5   Heat a frying pan over medium-low heat. Put the tortillas in one at a time. Cook each side for 3 minutes.

6   Put some of the apple mixture on each tortilla. Roll up the tortillas. Serve warm with a side of ice cream!

Cowboy Milk Fudge

A delicious delight everyone will love!

Makes 25 pieces

Ingredients

2 cups evaporated milk
1¾ cups sugar
¼ teaspoon ground cinnamon
3 tablespoons unsalted butter
1 teaspoon vanilla extract
½ cup chopped pecans
25 pecan halves

Tools

8 × 8-inch baking dish
waxed paper
measuring cups
measuring spoons
large saucepan
mixing spoon
candy thermometer
mixing bowl
sharp knife
rubber spatula
dinner knife

1   Line the baking dish with waxed paper.

2   Put the milk, sugar, cinnamon, and butter in a saucepan. Heat over medium-high heat. Stir frequently until the mixture reaches 240 degrees.

   Remove the pan from the heat. Pour the mixture into a mixing bowl. Stir in the vanilla and chopped pecans. Stir for 5 minutes. Be careful! The bowl might be hot.

   Pour the mixture into the baking dish. Spread evenly with a rubber spatula. Let cool 5 minutes. Press the pecan halves into the fudge.

5   Refrigerate until cool. Cut the fudge into pieces.

*hot!
*sharp!
*nuts!

Conclusion

Now you know how to make some wonderful Western dishes! Did you learn anything about Western **cuisine**? Did you try any new foods? Everywhere you go there are new foods to experience.

From coast to coast the United States is a land of **delicious** dishes! East Coast, Pacific Coast, Gulf Coast, Midwest, South, and West are the main regions of US cuisine. Try them all to get a taste of the United States. See if one is your favorite!

Glossary

burrito – a flour tortilla rolled or folded around a filling such as meat, cheese, and vegetables.

cuisine – a style of preparing and presenting food.

culture – the behavior, beliefs, art, and other products of a particular group of people.

delicious – very pleasing to taste or smell.

dessert – a sweet food, such as fruit, ice cream, or pastry, served after a meal.

grocery store – a store that sells mostly food items.

heritage – traditions or beliefs that are an important part of a group or country's history.

jerky – meat that has been cut into strips and dried so it won't spoil.

outdoorsy – related to or suitable for the outdoors.

permission – when a person in charge says it's okay to do something.

unique – different, unusual, or special.

utensil – a tool used to prepare or eat food.

versatile – having many uses.

version – a different form or type from the original.

Web Sites

To learn more about regional US cooking, visit ABDO Publishing Company online at www.abdopublishing.com. Web sites about easy and fun regional recipes are featured on our Book Links page. These links are routinely monitored and updated to provide the most current information available.

Index